Preface

I0116204

This book will wake you up from ignorance if you still believe in divinity and do not live science based bias of many issues. Scientist says that there was no science until few thousand years but they cannot prove how mega structures were built in Egypt, South America, Incas, and many places in India. This is irony that people still drinks many sodas like products knowing that it is dangerous and it has Brominated Vegetable Oil(BVO),which could be cancerous and a reason for many diabetes and diseases spreading all over world. This is science of consumerism not spiritual science; this is science of stock market not science of getting all people benefitted. I will start writing many series of books that could raise many controversies but that is needed to get out of ignorance.

COW A SACRED SCIENCE

Cows are considered just a meat by many non-Hindu people and it is unfortunate.

Cows, as '*Kamdhenu*' are the fulfiller of all desires. "*matrah sarva bhutanam, gavah sarv sukh prada*", Meaning, the cow being mother of all living entities gives all pleasures to everyone.

1) Cows receive auspicious rays from all heavenly constellations. Thus she contains influences of all constellations and thus universe. Wherever there is a cow, there is influence of all heavenly constellations; blessings of all gods. Cow is the only divine living being that has a Surya Ketu Nadi (nerve connected to sun) on her backbone absorbs Vitamin A. Therefore the cow's milk, butter and ghee have golden hue. Apart from Vitamin A, there are many unknown elements present in the cow's milk and cow's other bodily fluids which miraculously cures many diseases.

Ancient Santan/Hindu scripture state that "Suryaketu" nerve on cow's back absorbs harmful radiations and cleanses atmosphere. Mere presence of cows is a great contribution to environment.

Eyes are the window to the soul

Pure

Charaka Samhita states,

- "Milk is the best life strengthener."

-- While Casein protein in milk helps growth of infants,

-- Calcium and sulphur strengthen our bones.

-- Milk is also rich in vitamins D and B-complex.

- Yogurt arrests diarrhea, controls fat, and resists cancer.

- Ghee improves intelligence and beauty. It is used to treat eye diseases.

- Distilled cow urine is effective in treatment of flu, arthritis, bacterial diseases, food poisoning, indigestion, edema, and leprosy.

- Panchagavya Mix : Various Indian Ayurvedic medical formulations like Panchagavya Ghrita, Amritasara, Ghanavati, Ksharavati, Netrasara etc. are invaluable medicines in Ayurvedic system.

yatvagasthi gatam papam dehe tishthti mamke prasnat panchgavyasya dahasagnirivendhnam

Meaning : From skin to bones, whatever sins (diseases) are in my body, are destroyed by panchagavya just as fire destroys fuel.

3) In medicine: (In Ayurveda) it is said:

|| gavyam pavitram ca rasayanam ca pathyam ca hrdyam balam buddhi syataaayuh pradam rakt vikar hari tridosh hridrog vishapaham syata || Meaning : Cow urine panchgavya is great elixir, proper diet, pleasing to heart, giver of mental and physical strength, enhances longevity. It balances bile, mucous and airs. It helps in heart diseases and effect of poison. For thousands of years, people in India have used cow urine and cow dung for different purposes in their daily and ceremonial activities. Being highly recommended by the scriptures, it is considered safe to use.

Medicinal Benefits:

According to Ayurveda the cause of all diseases is the imbalance in three faults (tri-dosas) i.e. mucous, bile and air. Cow urine balances the tri-dosas, thus diseases are cured.

There are some micronutrients in our body, which give life strength. These micronutrients are flushed out through urine. Therefore gradually ageing steps in our body. Cow urine has all elements, which compensate for deficiency of nutrients in our body, which are required for healthy life.

Thus Cow urine stops ageing process. So it is called an elixir and also life giving.

(Urine & Cow Dung) provide the right solutions for most of the diseases that are considered incurable.

Cow urine has *Natural Disinfectant and Antiseptic* qualities. It helps in curing Cancer, AIDS, Asthma, Diabetes, High BP, Psoriasis, Eczema, Other Skin Diseases, Heart Diseases, Hypertension, Piles, Prostate, Liver, Kidney, Urinary Diseases, Female Diseases, Hepatitis, Acidity, Fits, Ulcer, Spleen, Ear, Sexual Disorders, Nose, Eye, Cough & Cold, Migraine, Headache, Gout, Knee Joint Pains, Sodalities, Sciatica and other chronic ailments.

Cow urine being miraculous poison destroyer, destroys the disease caused by poison (Toxin). Extremely dangerous chemicals are purified by cow urine. Cow urine provides immunity power by increasing resistance power against diseases in human body. It is anti-toxin.

Cow urine corrects functioning of liver. So, liver makes healthy pure blood. It gives disease resistance power to the body.

Cow urine contains many minerals especially copper, gold salts, etc. It compensates for bodily mineral deficiency. Presence of gold salts protects body against diseases.

Mental tension hurts nervous system. Cow urine is called medhya and hradya, which means it, gives strength to brain and heart. Thus cow urine protects heart and brain from damages caused by mental tension and protects these organs from disorders and diseases.

Excessive use of any medicine leaves some residue in our body. This residue causes diseases. Cow urine destroys the poisonous effects of residues and makes body disease free.

Electric currents (rays) which are present in the environment keep our body healthy. These rays in form of extremely small currents enter our body through Copper in our body. We get Copper from cow urine. To attract these electric waves is quality of Copper. Thus we become healthy.

By acting against the voice of soul (immoral & sinful action), the heart and mind become narrow minded. Due to this the functioning of body is effected and causes diseases. Cow urine provides mode of goodness. Thus helps us to perform correct activities by mind. Thus protects from diseases.

"Sarve rogaah hi mandagnau" All diseases begin with mandagni (Low fire i.e. digestive capacity). If fire is strong, diseases won't occur. Cow urine keeps the fire strong.

Irregular bowel movements cause diseases. Cow urine regulates bowel movements. Weakening of immunity system also causes disease. Cow urine is elixir. Gavyam tu samprotkam, jivaniya rasayanam meaning cow urine gives life and is elixir.

Bull's urine is stronger. But its medical value is no less as species is same. Just by smelling bull's urine, infertile woman can conceive child

In scriptures some diseases are said to be due to sinful actions performed in previous lives which we have to bear. Ganga resides in cow urine. Ganga is destroyer of sins, thus cow urine destroys such previous sins and so diseases are cured.

4) Organic colostrum benefits and rebuilds the human body at a deep foundational level. Asides from containing the building blocks (all the parent essential fatty acids, all the essential amino acids, etc for every nutrient needed by the body, the health benefits of colostrum milk can be attributed to these key compounds:

Naturally occurring IGF-1 (which stands for insulin-like growth factor 1) could be considered the crown jewel as to why cow colostrum benefits human longevity potential so well. According to Wikipedia, "IGF-1 is one of the most potent natural activators of the AKT signaling pathway, a stimulator of cell growth and proliferation, and a potent inhibitor of programmed cell death" (this helps combat the metabolic effects of aging). IGF-1 is one of the *many* growth factors found in bovine colostrum that helps create a state of anabolism in the body which can lead to increased lean muscle mass, bone density and tissue regeneration. The oligosaccharides that are present in colostrum benefit the healing of the skin externally in the form of reversing wrinkles and internally in the form of healing the lining of the digestive tract. These long chain sugars also serve as prebiotic and feed good bacteria in the intestine (including acidophilus) and aid in the maintenance of peak health for the digestive system.

Lacto peroxidase is an enzyme that acts as an anti-microbial agent. It is found naturally in milk and colostrum to prevent the proliferation of bad bacteria. These beneficial properties are then transferred over to those who consume it. Colostrum benefits your oral health if you let is dissolve in your mouth around your gums. This can prevent or even treat gingivitis and may be able to help re-grow a receding gum-line. Lacto peroxidase has also been shown to stimulate macrophages (white blood cells) to gobble up cancer cells present in the body.

The lactobacillus acidophilus in raw colostrum is a strain of healthy bacteria that is an important part of the human immune system. Many people develop an imbalance of not only their intestinal flora (healthy bacteria) but also the flora on their skin and other bodily orifices (ears, nose throat, mouth etc) over time due to poor diets and the use of medication and specifically antibiotics. Acidophilus taken orally in organic colostrum benefits the flora of the entire body by populating first the gut and then it eventually "overflows" into all other areas of the body. As previously mentioned, there are naturally occurring prebiotics in organic colostrum that feed acidophilus as well as any strains of good bacteria already present in your body.

Lactoferrin and hemopexin may be two key nutrients in "leveling the playing field" in terms of the difference of lifespan between men and women. One suspected cause for men living shorter live than women *on average* throughout the world is that they don't regularly shed their blood the way women do once a month. Iron is a pro-oxidant and the theory is that "rusty" old iron that is floating around the body for too long causes damage that builds up over time. Lactoferrin and hemopexin are known to bind to excess iron and remove it from the body safely.

Nucleosides found in dairy products and specifically in higher amounts in cow colostrum, have a number of beneficial functions for the body. Dietary nucleotides support immune modulation, meaning that they intelligently alter the immune system to become more effective, as opposed to just blatantly boosting it which may exacerbate underlying autoimmune conditions. These nutrients also enhance iron absorption in the digestive tract as well as help in the desaturation of fats, making them easier to digest!

Proline rich peptides (PRP's) act as hormones that regulate the thymus gland and help modulate the immune system (much in the same way as the nutrients mentioned above). Specifically, PRP's promote better functioning of T-lymphocytes, they help produce cytokines, they stimulate the activity of natural killer cells (NK cells) and they stimulate and modulate many other immunological functions. What makes cow colostrum one of the best antiaging foods is that PRP's increase the permeability of blood vessels in the skin, resulting in the improved uptake of nutrients into the skin which results in a healthier and more youthful complexion!

5) Cow dung has antiseptic, anti-radioactive and anti-thermal properties. When we coat the walls and clean the floors of house with cow dung, it protects the dwellers. In 1984, gas leak in Bhopal killed more than 20,000 people. Those living in houses with cow dung coated walls were not affected. Atomic power centers in India and probably Russia even today uses cow dung to shield radiation.

6) When we burn cow dung, it balances atmospheric temperature and kills germs in the air. We can also reduce acid content in water by treating it with cow dung.

7) When we offer ghee in fire as part of ritualistic sacrifices, it strengthens the ozone layer and shields the earth from harmful radiations from Sun.

8) Manures from cow urine & dung, makes the soil fertile, for yielding more nutrient fruits & Vegetables for healthy life. It Help in overcoming the negatives of Chemical fertilizers. 99% of the insects in nature are beneficial to the system. Insecticides prepared from cow urine or well fermented butter milk do not affect these helpful insects. Dung from one cow is adequate to fertilize 5 acres of land and its urine is can protect 10 acres of crop from insects. African deserts were made fertile using cow dung.

9) 70% of our people depend on agriculture. 98% of them depend on cattle based agriculture.

9) India has approximately 30 crore cattle. Using their dung to produce bio gas, we can save 6.0 crore ton of firewood every year. This would arrest deforestation to that extent.

Sadly its already important position is not accepted by our people.

Ghee, mixed with honey, is used for wounds, inflammation, and blisters. Ghee is salt and lactose free so it is a boon for those who can't drink milk or eat cheese. Ghee contains CLA or conjugated linoleic acid which aids weight loss, especially stubborn belly fat and has been . CLA is an antioxidant. Ghee is also very alkaline for your body, which helps to offset the overwhelming acidity of most modern junk food diets.

Ghee is full of Vitamins A, D, E, and K. These vitamins are fat-soluble, meaning they have to be digested with other fat molecules in order for these vitamins to make it into our bloodstream. Fortunately, ghee has lots of dietary fats (mostly saturated fats) that help our bodies absorb and make use of these vitamins.

Almost all fancy cooking oils like Soya, Sunflower, Safflower, Olive, Canola etc break down to produce deadly free radicals in high heat cooking. But ghee is an excellent cooking medium because it does not break down in high heat like these cooking oils do.).

It is better to cook with only the stable-at-high-temps oils like coconut, and ghee. Save the unstable olive oil for only salads, never cooking. Since ghee is lower in fat than butter, it's a better choice for people who have problems with high cholesterol. It is easier to digest. Because there is less fat in ghee,

Ghee can be stored for a long period of time, longer than butter can, and it doesn't need to be refrigerated when it is stored. This makes it more convenient than butter and better in some people's eyes.
Ghee contains both saturated and unsaturated fats. The total fat content of ghee consists of approximately 65 percent saturated fats, 25 percent monounsaturated and 5 percent polyunsaturated. Its saturated fat content consists of easily digested short-chain fatty acids for approximately 89 percent with an additional 3 percent from linoleic acid. This acid is a source of antioxidants that protect the body against free radicals and helps prevents serious health diseases such as heart disease and cancer.

COW A SACRED SCIENCE

Contrary of common belief, fats are essential to the diet. They help in normal body functions, hormonal balance, reproductive health, skin health and the absorption of essential vitamins. In particular, vitamins A, D, E and K are only able to be used by the body when they are taken with fats.

Ghee is beneficial in decreasing cholesterol in the blood. It does this by improving the ratio of HDL or good cholesterol, to LDL or the bad cholesterol. Increased HDL in the blood may decrease the risk of atherosclerosis and heart attacks.

Vedas have never been proved wrong as it was written by seers. When the Vedas talked about the power of an atom of the microcosm, all the West ridiculed it as cowherd's verses till one day the atom bomb shocked them out of their pants.

Today the scientists know that the copper used in the Agnihotra pyramids, resonates energy and send solutions into the ether of ZPF along with the OM quantum tunneling effect. Triangles have extraordinary energy.

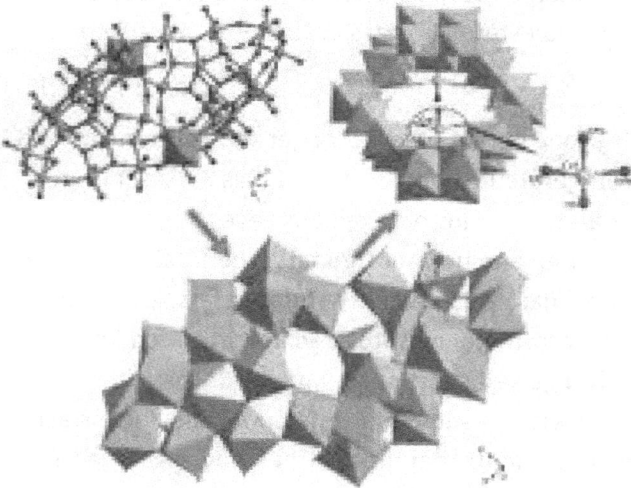

The NANO-molecular structure of copper is triangular.

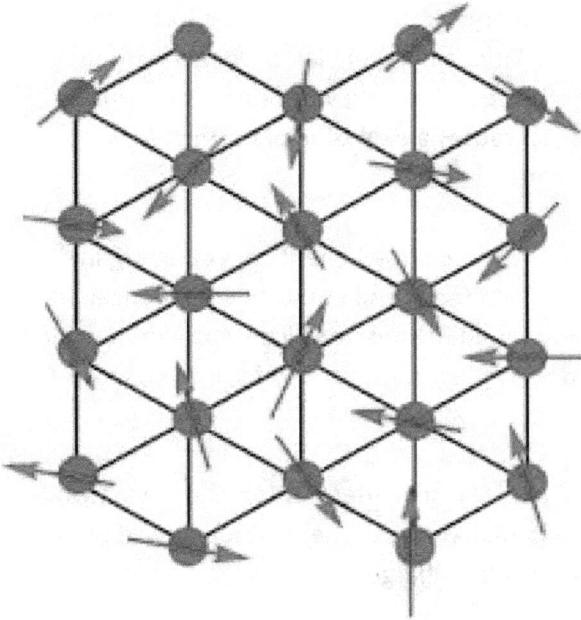

This was written down in our ancient Vedas. The Sri-Yantra which contains the theory of everything, the golden mean, the golden spiral and the magic cosmology number 108 is triangular.

Copper has anti-bacterial properties. The Vedic rishis always carried with them a copper lota containing living water. Copper is an excellent energy conductor, as we have seen in this modern electrical age. How is it that the seers knew this and wrote it down 7000 years ago?

People who do Agnihotra find it easy to go into the Alpha brainwave mode, which is creative. For women with PMS due to hormonal imbalances and a breakdown of the Ethereal body (aura) , this is a boon. Much pain can be avoided. The family who does it eliminated negativity. The reason why Vedas promoted Agnihotra at sunrise and sunset is because they understood the circadian rhythms and the flooding effect of abundant Prana or life force.

Kirlean cameras have proved that potted plants who were fed with Agnihotra ash had better bio-energy aura and colour. The fruits and organic vegetables had better Kirlean aura and lasted longer without getting rotten in a non-refrigerated space. No worms can breed inside these fruits. The Agnihotra ash causes a explosion of earth worms which bore the soil for oxygen to enter.

The Western world still does NOT know the benefits of eating organic food. They are destined to eat GM foods and get Alzheimer, Cancer and all sorts of negativity, bad habits, addictions and vices. They are destined to poison their fields with deadly pesticides, use food seeds which are sterile, and drink poisoned groundwater.

Cow dung has anti-bacterial penicillin like effect. This is the reason why agnihotra is effective on the human body. Viruses cannot survive on their own; they are parasites on weak low charge cells.

Ghee made from the Indian Punganur cow is good for Agnihotra. While cow milk normally has a fat content of 3 per cent, the Punganur breed's milk contains 8 per cent.

COW A SACRED SCIENCE

COW PROTECTION IN SANATAN DHARMA (HINDUISM) ~ the eternal code

Sanatan Dharma (सनातन धर्मं) is a divine code of conduct established by the dearest God. In it there are various Shrutis Smritis Dharma Shastras who glorify the divinity of cows & fruits of serving them. Cows (गऊ माता), are a symbol of abundance & all sanctity of life on earth that serves the beings like a mother without asking much in return. It is a part of Ancient traditions to avoid/ reject consumption of beef.

Hinduism is based on the concept of omnipresence of the Divine, and the presence of a soul in all creatures, including bovines. Thus, by that definition, killing any animal would be a sin: one would be obstructing the natural cycle of birth and death of that creature, and the creature would have to be reborn in that same form because of its unnatural death. Historically, even Krishna, one of the most revered forms of the Divine (Avatar), tended cows.

A Cow is said to be the abode of all the Gods,(means positive energy). As for education-God means positive energy and that is not a body or male or female per se.

Brahma and Vishnu on the root of two horns(positive energy of creation).

All the sacred reservoirs and Vedavyasa on the tips of the horns.

Lord Shankara on the centre head.

Parvathi on the edge of head.

Kartikeya on the nose, Kambala and Ashwatara Devas on the nostrils.

Ashwini Kumaras on the ears.

Sun and Moon in the eyes.

Vayu in dental range and Varuna on the tongue.

Saraswathi in the sound of cow.

COW A SACRED SCIENCE

Sandhya goddesses on the lips and Indra on the neck.

Raksha Ganas on the hanging under the neck.

Sadhya Devas in the heart.

Dharma on the thigh.

Gandharvas in the gap of hoofs, Pannaga at the tips, Apsaras on the sides.

Eleven Rudras and Yama on the back, Ashtavasus in the crevices.

Pitru Devas on the ides of umbilical joint, 12 Adityas on the stomach area.

Soma on the tail, Sun rays on the hair, Ganga in its urine, Lakshmi and Yamuna in the dung, Saraswathi in milk, Narmada in yogurt, and Agni in ghee

Prithwi in stomach, oceans in the udder, Kamadhenu in the whole body

Three Gunas in the root of the brows, Rishis in the pores of hair, and all the sacred lakes in the breathe.

Chandika on the lips and Prajapathi Brahma on the skin

Fragrant flowers on nostrils

Sadhya Devas on the arm-pit

Six parts of Vedas on the face, four Vedas on the feet, Yama on the top of the hoofs, Kubera and Garuda on the right, Yakshas on the left and Gandharvas inside

Khecharas in the fore of the foot, Narayana in intestine, mountains in the bones, Artha, Dharma, Kama and Moksha in the feet.

Four Vedas in the Hoom... sound

COW A SACRED SCIENCE

There are 7 mothers listed in scriptures. They are...

'adau mata guru-patni, brahmani raja-patnika dhenur dhatri tatha prthvi saptaita matarah' Meaning:

Real mother & Guru-patni, the wife of spiritual master or teacher. Brahmani, the wife of a brahmana, and Raja-patnika, the queen. Dhenu, the cow, Dhatri, nurse, as well as theEarth. Earth is mother because she gives us so many things like fruits, flowers, grains for our eating. Mother gives milk & food for eating. Cow gives us milk. So cow is also one of our mothers.

SCRIPTURE SPEAK :

1) SRIMAD BHAGVAD GITA

Dhenunam asmi kamadhuk -- Among cows I am the wish fulfilling (kamdhenu or surabhi) cow. (Verse 10.28).

2) SRI CHAITANYA CHARITAMRITA, Adilila, Chapter 17, verse 166,

Caitanya Mahaprabhu confirms:

o-ange yata loma tata sahasra vatsara go-vadhi raurava-madhye pace nirantar

Cow killers and cow eaters are condemned to rot in hell for as many thousands of years as there are for each hair on the body of every cow they eat from.

It is further written - Those who fail to give cows reverence and protection and choose to foolishly oppose and whimsically ignore the injunctions of the Vedic scriptures by selling a cow for slaughter, by killing a cow, by eating cows flesh and by permitting the slaughter of cows will all rot in the darkest regions of hell for as many thousands of years as there are hairs on the body of each cow slain. There is no atonement for the killing of a cow.

3) *MANU SAMHITA, chapter 4, verse 162 :*

A guru, a teacher, a father, a mother, a Brahmana(means who gives knowledge), a cow and a yogi all should never be killed.

धर्मो रक्षत रक्षतिः - मनु कहते हैं- जो धर्म की रक्षा करता है धर्म उसकी रक्षा करता है । सत्य से धर्म की रक्षा होती है ।

4) Shri Brahm Samhita 5.29 :

cintāmaṇi-prakara-sadmasu kalpa-vṛkṣa- lakṣāvṛteṣu

surabhir abhipālayantam lakṣmī-sahasra-śata-sambhrama-

sevyamānaṁ govindam ādi- puruṣaṁ tam ahaṁ bhajāmi

I worship Govinda, the primeval Lord, the first progenitor who is tending the cows, yielding all desire, in abodes built with spiritual gems, surrounded by millions of purpose trees, always served with great reverence and affection by hundreds of thousands of lakṣmīs or gopīs.

5) *SHRI RAMCHARITMANAS*

Vedas & Devatas in their prayer Jai Jai Surnayak describe the lord as " Go Dvij Hitkari (protector of cows & Brahmins) Jai Asurari (Death for Wrongdoers) "

6) *MAHABHARATA,*

Anusasana-parva, 115.43 -116.45: *That wretch among men who pretending to follow the path of righteousness prescribed in the Vedas, would kill living creatures from greed of flesh would certainly go to hellish regions.*

Anusasana-parva, 114.6, 115.6 it states: *As the footprints of all moving, living beings are engulfed in those of the elephant, even thus all religions are to be understood by ahimsa which is non-violence to any living being by thought, words or actions.*

गवां मूत्रपुरीषस्य नोद्वजित कथंचन । न चासां मांसमश्नीयाद्गवां पुष्टि
तथाप्नुयात् ॥ (Mahabharata, Anushasana Parva 78-17)

Do not hesitate to consume cow urine and cow dung – they are sacred. But one should never eat the cow meat. A person becomes stronger by consuming Panchagavya.

गावो ममाग्रतो नतियं गावः पृष्ठत एव च । गावो मे सर्वतश्चैव गवां
मध्ये वसाह्यहम् ॥ (Mahabharata, Anushasana Parva 80-3)

Let there be cows in front of me, behind me and all around me. I live with the cows.

दानानामपि सर्वेषां गवां दानं प्रशस्यते । गावः श्रेष्ठाः पवित्राश्च पावनं
ह्येतदुत्तमम् ॥ (Mahabharata, Anushasana Parva 83-3)

Donation of cows is superior to all others. Cows are supreme and sacred.

COW IN VEDAS: In the Vedas, Cow is called Aditi, Dhenuvu, Aghnaaya etc. 'Cow is refered in the Rg Veda 723 times, in Yajurveda 87 times, In Sama Veda 170 times, in Athrava Veda 331 times-total 1331 times. Similarly 20 times in Rg Veda, 5 times in Yajurveda, 2 times in Sama veda and 33 times in Athrava veda the word Aghnaaya specifically addressed to cow. "Dhenu" is used 76 times in Rg Veda, 22 times in Yajurveda, 25 times in Sama Veda, 43 times in Atharva Veda. The meaning of Dhenu is which gives Trupti (Contentment and satisfaction).

7) RIG VEDA:

Cattle were important to Rig Vedic people & several hymns refer to more than ten thousand cattle.

Rig Veda 7.95.2. and other verses (e.g. 8.21.18) also mention that the Sarasvati region poured milk and "fatness" (ghee), indicating that cattle were herded in this region.

In the Rig Veda, the cows figure frequently as symbols of wealth, and also in comparison with river goddesses, e.g. in 3.33.1cd, *Like two bright mother cows who lick their young, Vipas and Sutudri speed down their waters.*

In X.87.16 we find: One who partakes of human flesh, the flesh of a horse or of another animal and deprives others from milk by slaughtering cows ; if such a fiend does not desist then even cut off their heads by your powers Oh king.

According to Aurobindo, in the Rig Veda the cows sometimes symbolize "light" and "rays". Aurobindo wrote that Aditi (the supreme Prakriti/Nature force) is described as a cow, and the Deva or Purusha (the supreme being/soul) as a bull.

The Vedic god Indra is often compared to a bull. Rivers are often likened to cows in the Rigveda, Vyasa said: *Cows are sacred. They are embodiments of merit. They are high and most efficacious cleansers of all.*

८.१०१.१५ – मैं समझदार मनुष्य कोकहे देता हूँ की तू बेचारी बेकसूर गायकी हत्या मत कर, वह अदिति हैं अर्थात काटने- चीरने योग्य नहीं हैं.।

८.१०१.१६ – मनुष्य अल्पबुद्धि होकर गाय को मारे कांटे नहीं.

६.२८.४ – गोए वधालय में न जाये

Cow â€" The aghnya â€" brings us health and prosperity. 1.164.27)

There should be excellent facility for pure water for Aghnya Cow. (5.83.8)

COW A SACRED SCIENCE

The Aghnya cows â€" which are not to be killed under any circumstancesâ€" may keep themselves healthy by use of pure water and green grass, so that we may be endowed with virtues, knowledge and wealth. (Rigveda 1.164.40 or Atharv 7.73.11 or Atharv 9.10.20)

The entire 28th Sukta or Hymn of 6th Mandal of Rigveda sings the glory of cow.

~ 1) Everyone should ensure that cows are free from miseries and kept healthy.

~ 2) God blesses those who take care of cows.

~ 3) Even the enemies should not use any weapon on cows

~ 4) No one should slaughter the cow

~ 5) Cow brings prosperity and strength

~ 6) If cows keep healthy and happy, men and women shall also keep disease free and prosperous

~ 7) May the cow eat green grass and pure water. May they not be killed and bring prosperity to us.

8) ATHARVA VEDA

Cow's body is represented by various devas and other subjects.

In VIII.6.23 we find: Those who eat cooked or uncooked flesh, who eat eggs and embryos are following an evil addiction that must be put to an end.

It is definitely a great sin to kill innocents. Do not kill our cows, horses and people. -- 10.1.29

Oh Goddess cow you make a weak person strong,you make a glowless person beautiful and not only that you-; you with your auspicious sounds make our homes auspicious. {4.21}

१२.४.३८ -जो (वृद्ध) गाय को घर में पकाता हैं उसके पुत्र मर जाते हैं.

४.११.३- जो बैलो को नहीं खाता वह कसत में नहीं पड़ता हैं

७.५.५ – वे लोग मूढ़ हैं जो कुत्ते से या गाय के अंगों से यज्ञ करते हैं

आ गावो अग्मन्नुत भद्रकम्रन् सीदंतु गोष्मेरणयंतवस्मे । परजावतीः
पुरुरूपा इहस्सयुरद्रिाय पूर्वीरुष्सोदुहानाः ॥

यूयं गावो मे दयथा कृशं चद्शिरीरं चत्किृणुथा सुप्रतीकम् । भद्र गृहं
कृणुथ भद्रवाचो बृहद्वो वय उच्यते सभासु ॥

Oh Cows! With your milk and ghee you make the physically weak strong, and nurture the sick to health. With your sacred utterances, you chastise our homes. Your glory is discussed in gatherings. (Atharvana Veda 4-21-11 and 6)

वशां देवा उपजीवंति वशां मनुष्या उप । वशेदं सर्वं भवतु यावतु सूर्यो
वपिश्यति ॥

The Gods and men live on cow products. Till the Sun shines, the universe will have Cows. The whole universe depends on the support of cow.

(Atharvana Veda 10-10-34)

9) YAJUR VEDA

A human being should not kill Cows & other animals & should ensure nobody else does --12.73

Do not kill cows and bulls who always deserve to be protected. -- 13.49

Destroy those who kill cows.-- 30.18 - गोहत्यारे को पुराण दंड दो

You must not use your God-given body for killing
God's (*innocent)creatures,whether they are human, animal or whatever.

सा वश्विायूः सा वश्विकरुमा सा वश्विधायाः।   (Shulka Yajurveda 1-4)

That cow would augment the life span of the sages involved in the
sacrifices and the doer of the sacrifices. Cow coordinates all the rituals of
the sacrifices. By providing offerings like milk, cow nourishes all the Gods
of the sacrifices.

10) HARIVAMSHA PURAN

The Harivamsha depicts Krishna as a cowherd. He is often described as
Bala Gopala, "the child who protects the cows." Another of Krishna's
names, Govinda, means "one who brings satisfaction to the cows." Other
scriptures identify the cow as the "mother" of all civilization, its milk
nurturing the population. The gift of a cow is applauded as the highest
kind of gift.

The milk of a cow is believed to promote Sattvic (purifying) qualities.
The ghee (clarified butter) from the milk of a cow is used in ceremonies
and in preparing religious food. Cow dung is used as fertilizer, as a fuel
and as a disinfectant in homes.

11) PURANAS

The earth-goddess Prithvi was, in the form of a cow, successively milked
of various beneficent substances for the benefit of humans, by various
deities.

गावो बंधुरमनुष्याणां मनुष्याबांधवा गवाम् । गौः यस्मनि् गृहेनास्ति
तद्बंधुरहतिं गृहम् ॥   (Padmapurana)

Cows are the abode of the Goddess of wealth. Sins don't touch them. There exists a fine relationship between man and cow. A home without a cow is like one without dear ones.

12) SRIMAD BHAGVATAM,

(Canto 11, chapter 5, verse 14 :5) "Those who are ignorant of the absolute truth and believe they are virtuous although wicked and arrogant who kill animals without any feeling of remorse or fear of punishment are devoured by those very same animals in their next birth."

(Chapter 8, 8.2)   tām agni-hotrīm ṛṣayo jagṛhur brahma-

vādinaḥ yajñasya deva-yānasya medhyāya haviṣe nṛpa

O King Parīkṣit, great sages who were completely aware of the Vedic ritualistic ceremonies took charge of that surabhi cow, which produced all the yogurt, milk and ghee absolutely necessary for offering oblations into the fire. They did this just for the sake of pure ghee, which they wanted for the performance of sacrifices to elevate themselves to the higher planetary systems, up to Brahmaloka.

(Canto 8: Chapter 24, Text 5) BRAHMINICAL CULTURE CANNOT BE MAINTAINED WITHOUT COW PROTECTION" . Without protection of cows, brahminical culture cannot be maintained; and without brahminical culture, the aim of life cannot be fulfilled.

13) GAVOPANISHADA:

Text Two: gävo bhütäm ca bhävyaà cagävah pustih sanätanégävo laksmäs tathä mülaàgoñu dattam na naçyati

"The cow is the past and future. She nourishes the health of all living entities, and she is the root of prosperity. The piety one achieves by feeding a cow in never destroyed."

Text Three   annaà hy paramam gävodevänää paramaà haviùsvähakära vañaö käraugoñu nityaà pratiñöhitau

"The cow is the cause of one's accumulation of food grains. She awards the best sacrificial ingredients to the demigods. The sacrifice of the demigods and the sacrifice of Indra are both performed on the basis of the cow."

Text Four   gävo yajïasya hy phalaàgoñu yajnah pratiñöhitahgävo bhaviçyaà bhütaà cagoñu -yajïäù pratiñöhitaù

"It is the cow which awards the result of sacrifice. The performance of sacrifice is dependent upon her. She is the past and future. All sacrifices are based upon her."

Text Five   säyaà prätaçca satataàhoma käle mahädyutegävo dadati vai homyamåñibhyaù puruñarsabha

"O greatly powerful King, every morning and evening when the sages perform fire sacrifices, it is the cow who supplies them the essential ingredients, in the form of ghee, etc."

Text Six   yäni käni ca durgäniduñkåtäni kåtäni cataranti caiva papmänaàdhenuà ye dadati prabho

"My dear King, those who give milk-cows in charity become liberated from all types of danger, and also become free from all sinful reactions."

Text Eleven   nä kértayitvä gäha supyättäsää saàsmrtyä cotpatetsäyää prätar namasye cagästataù pustimäpnuyät

"Do not go to bed at night without praising cows. Do not get up in the morning without remembering the cow. Offer respect to the cow daily, in the morning. By doing so, a human being achieves strength and nourishment."

Text Twelve   gavää mütra purisasyanodvijeta kathaïcanana cäsää määsa maçnéyädgavää pustià tathäpnuyät

"Do not hate cow urine and cow dung. Never eat cow meat. By following this advice, human beings can become prosperous."

Text Thirteen   gäçca sankértaye nityaànäva manyeta tästathäanistaà svapramälaksyagää naraù samprakértayet

"Chant the name of the cow daily and never insult her. If one sees a bad dream, one should immediately remember the cow."

Text Fifteen   ghåtena juhuyädagnighåtena svasti väcayetghåtaà dadyät ghåtaà präçodgavää pustià sadäçnute

"Use ghee in fire sacrifices. Use ghee in all auspicious activities. Donate ghee and also use it for personal necessities. By doing this, the human beings will always support the cows and understand their value.

Text Seventeen   gävo maàupatisthantuhema çrìgyäh payo mucahsurahu saurabhe yaççasaritah sägaraà yathä

"As the rivers flow into the ocean, may Surabhi and Saurabheyi cows that give milk and have horn covered with gold, come to me."

Text Twenty   gävää dåñövä namaskåtyakuryäcciva pradakñinaàpradakiñné kåtä tenasaptadvipä vasundharä

mätarah sarva bhütänäàgävah sarva sukha pradähvåddhià äkaàçatä nityaàgävah käryäh pradakñinäh

"One should see, offer obeisances, and circumambulate the cow. By doing so, one is suppose to have circumambulated the entire earth, with its seven islands. The cow is the mother of all. She gives happiness to everyone. People who desire prosperity should daily circumambulate the cow."

14) Rik Samhita

यः पौरुषेण क्रविषा समंक्ते यो अश्वेन पशुना यातुधानः । ये अघ्न्याये भरतकि षीरमग्ने तेषां शीर्षाणि हरसापि वृश्चः ॥ (Rik Samhita 87 – 161)

Oh fire god, with your flames burn the heads of those demons who eat the meat of humans, animals like horse and cow, and those who steal cows' milk.

प्रजापतर्रिमह्यमेता रराणो विश्वैर्देवैः पितृभिः संविदानः । शिवाः सतीरुप नो गोष्ठमाकस्तासां वयं प्रजया संसदेम ॥ (Rik Samhita 10 – 169 – 4)

May the supreme Lord, complemented by all the Gods, create auspicious and spacious cowsheds for our happiness and populate them with cows and calves. Let us rejoice the cow-wealth and contend by serving those cows.

15) Other Quotes:

सा नो मंद्रेषमूरजम् दुहाना । धेनुर्वा गस्मानुष सुष्टुतैतु ॥

She is Kamadhenu – the divine cow that fulfils all our desires. Her body is of cow and face is of a woman. She was born before the amrutha when the ocean was churned. Her hair exudes fragrance. From her udder she showers Dharma, Artha, Kama and Moksha. She is an abode to self-knowledge, shelters, Sun, Moon and Fire God. All the Gods and the living beings depend on her. She provides us with food and supreme knowledge even when we mildly pray. Let her be near us.

पीतोदका जग्धतृणा दुग्धदेहा निरिंद्रियाः । आनंदा नाम तेलोकसतान् स गच्चत्ति ता ददत् ॥

These cows have eaten grass and have taken water. They have been milked. They are past reproductive age. One who donates these old cows will go to place of darkness devoid of pleasures. Instead, donate me. (Kathopanishat – Nachiketa tells sage Vajashravas during Vishwajit Yaga)

पार्थो वत्सः सुधीर्भोक्तादुग्धं गीतामृतः महत् ॥

Bhagavad-Gita is the essence of Upanishads. It is like a cow whom Srikrishna milks. Arjuna is like a calf. The learned devotees are drinking the ambrosial milk of Bhagavad-Gita.

गौर्मे माता वृषभः पिता मे दिवं शर्म जगते मे परतिष्ठा ।

Cow is my mother and ox my father. Let the pair bless me with happiness in this world and bliss in heaven. I depend on cow for my life – thus stating one should surrender to cow.

वागिंद्रियिसवरूपायै नमः । वाचावृत्ततपिरद्ददयनिये नमः ॥ अकारादक्षिकारांतवैखरीवक्सवरूपणिये नमः ॥ (Atri Samhita 310)

By the service of the cow and consuming cow products, awareness and spirit, both enhance.

यन्न वेदध्वनधि़यांतं न च गोभरिलंकृतम् ।   यन्नबालैः परवृितं
श्मशानमवि तद्गृहम् ॥   (Vishnusmriti)

The house where Vedas are not chanted, where cows are not seen where
children are not around it is like a graveyard.

गोमूत्रगोमयं सर्पि क्षीरं दधि च रोचना । षदंगमेतत् परमं मांगल्यं
सर्वदा गवाम् ॥

Cow's urine, dung, milk, ghee, curd and gorochana – these six are the
most auspicious products.

एक गाय अपने जीवन काल में 4,10,440 मनुष्यों हेतु एक समय का
भोजन जुटाती है, जब की उस के मांस से 80 मांसाहारी केवल एक समय में
अपना पेट भर सकते हैं ! -: स्वामी दयानंद सरस्वती (गो करुना नधि़
कतिाब में से)

****

16) COW PROTECTION IN SIKH SECT:

उग्रदन्ती ~~

यही दे हु आज्ञा तुरकन गहि खपाऊं !गऊ घात का दोख जगसों
मटिाऊं।~~ हे मां भवानी, मुझे आशीर्वाद और आदेश द'कि धर्म वरिोधी
अत्याचारी तुर्कों को चुन-चुनकर समाप्त कर दूं और इस जगत से
गौहत्या का कलंक मिटि दूं।~ गुरु गोवन्दि सहि जी

सकल जगत मो खालसा पंथ गाजै,जगै धरम हिन्दुक तुरक दुंद भाजै।~~
सारे जगत में खालसा पंथ की गूंज हो, हिन्दू धर्म का उत्थान हो तथा
तुर्कों द्वारा पैदा की गयी विपत्तियां समाप्त हों।

ਨਾਮਾ ਪ੍ਰਣਵੈ ਮੇਲ ਮਮੇਲ ॥नामा प्रणवै सेल मसेल ॥ ~~~ Nāmā paraṇvai
sėl masėl. Naam Dayv prayed, and milked the cow. Page 1166, Line 6

ਹਮ ਗੋਰੂ ਤੁਮ ਗੁਆਰ ਗੁਸਾਈ ਜਨਮ ਜਨਮ ਰਖਵਾਰੇ ॥हम गोरू तुम गुआर गुसाई
जनम जनम रखवारे ॥ Ham gorū ṯum gu*ār gusā*ī janam janam rakẖvārė.
~~~ I am a cow, and You are the herdsman, the Sustainer of the World.
You are my Saving Grace, lifetime after lifetime. Devotee Kabir -Page 482,
Line 13

ਕਾਮਧੇਨ ਹਰਿ ਹਰਿ ਗੁਣ ਗਾਮ ॥कामधेन हरि हरि गुण गाम ॥Kāmḏẖėn har har
guṇ gām.The Khaamadhayn, the cow of miraculous powers, is the singing
of the Glory of the Lord's Name, Har, Har. --Guru Arjan Dev, Page 265,
Line 5

मांस की प्राप्ति तभी संभव है जब दूसरे जीवों का वध किया जाये,
लेकिन जीव हिंसा करने से स्वर्ग नहीं मिलता इसलिए सुख तथा स्वर्ग
को पाने की कामना रखने वाले द्विज को मांस भक्षण त्याग देना
चाहिए ।199।

मांस की उत्पत्ति और जीवों के बंधन तथा वध को समझकर सभी
प्रकार के मांस भक्षण को त्याग देना चाहिए ।200।

वे सभी जीव वध के लिए समान रूप से दोषी हैं जो जीव वध की
अनुमति देते हैं, जीव के अंगों को काट कर अलग अलग करते हैं, उसका

वध करते हैं, उसको बेचते हैं, उसको खरीदते हैं, उसको पकाते हैं, उसको परोसते हैं, और उसको खाते हैं ।201।

मुनियों के बीच रहते हुए उनकी तरह से सात्विक कंद मूल तथा फल का भोजन करने से वह पुण्य फलप्राप्त नहीं होता, जो केवल मांसाहार के त्याग से मिलता है ।202।

विद्वानों के अनुसार मांस शब्द मां, तथा स, शब्दों के योग से बना है इसका अर्थ होता है- जिसे मैं इस संसार में खाता हूँ, वही मुझे परलोक में खाये ।203।

"Don't give your animals in the hands of butchers." - SatPurush Baba Fulsande Wale

Guru Govind Singh, the 10th Guru, told Pandit Prithwiraj that Khalsa sect was established to care for the economy, right behaviour, cows, Brahmins, and protection of the down-trodden.

Guru Govind Singh's first Guru was against killing of any animal – not only cows.

In 1871, under the leadership of Guru Rama Singh, 3,15,000 Sikhs participated in an agitation against the British to get the slaughter houses closed.

****

17) COW PROTECTION IN BUDDHISM SECT

Gautam Buddha preached about the utility & importance of cows. He advocated against Cow Slaughter & gave importance on cow rearing.

यथा माता सति भ्राता अज्ञे वापि च ज्ञातका । गावो मे परमा मतिता
यातु जजायंति औषधा ॥ अन्नदा बलदा चेता वण्णदा सुखदा तथा
। एतवत्थवसं ज्ञत्वा नास्सुगावो हनि सुते ॥

Like parents, siblings, members of family and community, cow is dear to us. It is very helpful. We prepare medicine from its milk. Cow gives food, strength, beauty, and pleasure. Similarly ox supports family men. We should treat the ox and cow like our parents.

~~(Goutama Budha)

गोहाणि सख्य गहिनं पोसका भोगरायका । तस्मा हि माता पति व मानये
सक्करेय्य च ॥ १४ ॥ ये च खादंति गोमांसं मातुमासं व खादये ॥ १५ ॥

Cows and oxen provide necessary and appropriate products to all households. Therefore we should treat them with care and respect like we treat our parents. Eating cow's meat is like eating one's own mother's flesh. (Lokaneeti 7)

"Let all creatures, let all things that live, all beings of whatever kind, see nothing that will bode them ill! May naught of evil come to them!" ~~ Buddha (quoted in the Culla-Vagga)

The Mahayana tradition is especially strong on vegetarianism; it pictures the Buddha not only as himself a vegetarian, but as one who taught others to be vegetarians. The Lankavatara sutra devotes an entire chapter to the evils of eating meat, saying:
"Meat eating in any form, in any manner, and in any place is unconditionally and once for all prohibited. . . . Meat eating I have not permitted to anyone, I do not permit, I will not permit."

All beings hate pains; therefore one should not kill them. This is the quintessence of wisdom: not to kill anything. ~~Sutrakritanga

"I do not see any reason why animals should be slaughtered to serve as human diet when there are so many substitutes. After all, man can live without meat..."

Many Buddha temples in Thailand have idols of cows. A cow idol occupies a prominent location in the world famous Buddha temple in Bangkok.

****

18) COW PROTECTION IN JAIN SECT

The cow was accorded top priority in Jain sect and in fact, the cow was the symbol of the first Jain Teerthankar Adinathji Maharaj.

In the life of a Jain saint the cow bore immense respect and significance.

सभी प्राणियों के दर्द से नफरत है, इसलिए उन्हें मार नहीं चाहिए ! इस ज्ञान का सारतत्व है: किसी भी प्राणी, जीव कि हत्या मत करो -- Sutrakritanga (जैन धर्म)

Those who have forsaken the killing of all; those who are helpmates to all; those who are a sanctuary to all; those men are in the way of heaven. ~~~ Hitopadesa

When Jainism flourished, they were active in cow protection. They built huge cowsheds and made cow rearing part of their lifestyle. Cruelty against cows, starving them, overloading, mutilating their body were all prohibited by law.

Mahaveera had ordered his disciples to rear 60,000 cows.

When Ananda became a disciple of Mahaveera, he vowed to run 8 Gokulas. One Vraja/Gokula = 10,000 cows. Ten citizens who owned maximum cows were named "Rajagriha Mahashataka" and "Kashiyachulanipita." One's wealth was assessed by the number of cows he possessed.

****

19) SCRIPTURES OF PAGANISM

Classical paganism had many illustrious vegetarians who were outspoken on the subject. Such figures as Ovid, Appolonius of Tyana, Plutarch, Plotinus, and Porphyry were all vegetarians who also identified themselves with classical paganism.

Plutarch's essay

On Eating of Flesh is still quoted by vegetarians today. Porphyry, living several hundred years later, wrote the earliest surviving book- length treatment of vegetarianism, *On Abstinence from Animal Food,* where he forthrightly deals with the moral worth of animals, the natural repugnance of humans to animal flesh, and the effects of meat-eating on health.

Many modern neo-pagans are vegetarians as well, as is evident from looking at modern neo-pagan literature. They quote the Pagan Federation principles in support of their vegetarianism: "`Do what you will, but harm none.'

****

20) COW PROTECTION IN JUDAISM SECT:

They base their vegetarianism on the fact that the first diet commanded by God in Genesis was a vegetarian diet: "God also said, 'I give you all plants that bear seed everywhere on earth, and every tree bearing fruit which yields seed: they shall be yours for food.'" (Genesis 1:29). The ultimate desire of God is for a world like that in the Garden of Eden, where humans and even animals are all vegetarian:

"The wolf shall dwell with the lamb, and the leopard shall lie down with the kid, and the calf and the lion and the fatling together, and a little child shall lead them. . . . They shall not hurt or destroy in all my holy mountain; for the earth shall be full of the knowledge of the Lord as the waters cover the sea." (Isaiah 11:6, 9)

Compassion to animals is part of Jewish teaching. Animals, as well as humans, are to be rested on the sabbath (Exodus 20:10), one has an obligation to relieve the suffering of animals (Deuteronomy 22:4, Exodus 23:5), and "a righteous man cares for his beast" (Proverbs 12:10). God himself cares for animals, for "his tender care rests upon all his creatures" (Psalms 145:9).

Finally, Proverbs 23:20 advises, "Be not among winebibbers, or among gluttonous eaters of meat."

****

21) COW PROTECTION IN CHRISTIANITY:

Many early Christians were vegetarian,

including Clement of Alexandria, Origen, John Chrysostom, Jerome, and Basil the Great.

According to some early church writings,

Matthew, Peter, and James the brother of Jesus were vegetarians. Many of the Old Testament principles concerning compassion for animals are accepted by Christians. God's compassion for animals is indicated at several points in the New Testament as well: Luke 12:6 states,"Are not five sparrows sold for two pennies? And not one of them is forgotten before God." Matthew 12:7 states about animal sacrifice: "If you had known what that text means, `I require mercy, not sacrifice,' you would not have condemned the innocent."

Old Testament of the Bible which applies to both Christians and Jews in Issaih, chapter 66 verse 3:

"He that killeth an ox is as if he slew a man. He that sacrifices a lamb is as if he slit a dogs neck, he that offereth it as an oblation is as if he offered swines blood, he that burneth it as incense as if he blessed an idol. Yea they have chosen their way and their soul delighteth in their abominations."

Modern day Christian vegetarians include many in the Seventh-day Adventist church, which recommends vegetarianism to its members, and the great humanitarian Albert Schweitzer, who said:

"While so much ill-treatment of animals goes on, while the moans of thirsty animals in railway trucks sound unheard, while so much brutality prevails in our slaughterhouses . . . we all bear guilt. Everything that lives has value as a living thing, as one of the manifestations of the mystery that is life."

****

22) SCRIPTURES OF BAHAY RELIGION:

The Baha'i writings do not specifically forbid meat or require vegetarianism. However, it is safe to say that vegetarianism is strongly encouraged. The Baha'i writings state:

"The food of the future will be fruit and grains. The time will come when meat will no longer be eaten. . . . our natural food is that which grows out of the ground. The people will gradually develop up to the condition of this natural food."

"To blessed animals the utmost kindness must be shown, the more the better. Tenderness and loving-kindness are basic principles of God's heavenly Kingdom. Ye should most carefully bear this matter in mind."

"It is not only their fellow human beings that the beloved of God must treat with mercy and compassion, rather must they show forth the utmost loving-kindness to every living creature. For in all physical respects, and where the animal spirit is concerned, the selfsame feelings are shared by animal and man. . . . The feelings are one and the same, whether ye inflict pain on man or on beast."

"Train your children from their earliest days to be infinitely tender and loving to animals."

-- Keith Akers

****

23) COW PROTECTION IN ZOROASTRIANS:

Zoroaster prayed to God for knowledge and conduct to achieve prosperity of cows and human kind. (Yashana 4512)

****

Important links:
1)http://eng.gougram.org/cow-urine-medicine/research/
2)http://www.gomataseva.org/faq/
3)http://www.iscowp.org/practical-benefits.html
4) http://ajitvadakayil.blogspot.com
5) http://ayurveda-foryou.com/archive/homa.html

www.ingramcontent.com/pod-product-compliance
Lightning Source LLC
Chambersburg PA
CBHW060531280326
41933CB00014B/3134